THE GREAT BOOKS FOUNDATION
Discussion Guide *for* Teachers

INDIVIDUAL RIGHTS

About Perfection Learning

Founded by two educators, Perfection Learning is a family-owned company that has provided innovative, effective reading, literature, and language arts materials to K–12 classroom teachers for more than eighty-five years. The company offers two flagship literature programs, *Literature & Thought* and *Many Voices,* through its partnership with the Great Books Foundation. Each program uses engaging, thought-provoking literature selections to teach middle and high school students to be critical readers and thinkers. Each anthology is structured to help students explore essential questions and develop the skills necessary to be successful in the twenty-first century.

About the Great Books Foundation

The Great Books Foundation is an independent, nonprofit educational organization whose mission is to empower readers of all ages to become more reflective and responsible thinkers. To accomplish this, the Foundation teaches the art of civil discourse through Shared Inquiry™ and publishes enduring works of literature across the disciplines.

The Great Books Foundation was established in 1947 to promote liberal education for the general public. In 1962, the Foundation extended its mission to children with the introduction of Junior Great Books®. Since its inception, the Foundation has helped thousands of people throughout the United States and in other countries begin their own discussion groups in schools, libraries, and community centers. Today, Foundation instructors conduct hundreds of professional learning courses for teachers and parents each year, and Great Books programs help more than one million students learn to read, discuss, and appreciate some of the world's most enduring literature. Great Books programs combine classroom materials and the Shared Inquiry method of learning to provide the essential elements that students need to meet and surpass the goals of the Common Core State Standards for English Language Arts.

THE GREAT BOOKS FOUNDATION
Discussion Guide *for* Teachers

INDIVIDUAL RIGHTS
THE BLESSINGS OF LIBERTY

Perfection Learning

The Great Books Foundation
A nonprofit educational organization

Shared Inquiry™ is a trademark of the Great Books Foundation. Junior Great Books® is a registered trademark of the Great Books Foundation. The contents of this publication include proprietary trademarks and copyrighted materials and may be used or quoted only with permission and appropriate credit to the Foundation.

Copyright © 2012 by The Great Books Foundation
Chicago, Illinois
All rights reserved
ISBN 978-1-933147-89-5

First printing
1 2 3 4 5 6 PP 17 16 15 14 13 12
Printed in the United States of America

Published and distributed by

The Great Books Foundation
A nonprofit educational organization
35 East Wacker Drive, Suite 400
Chicago, IL 60601

www.greatbooks.org

Contents

ABOUT SHARED INQUIRY AND THIS GUIDE — 7

SCHEDULING SHARED INQUIRY ACTIVITIES — 8

CONDUCTING SHARED INQUIRY ACTIVITIES — 10
- Prereading — 10
- First Reading — 10
- Sharing Questions — 11
- Second Reading — 12
- Shared Inquiry Discussion — 14
- Writing After Discussion — 17

ASSESSMENT AND REFLECTION — 18

SELECTIONS

GEORGE WASHINGTON AND THE TOURO SYNAGOGUE — 20
and **JEFFERSON AND THE "WALL OF SEPARATION"** *letters*
Moses Seixas/George Washington *and* Thomas Jefferson

THOUGHTS THAT WE HATE *book* — 22
Anthony Lewis

THE SPIRIT OF LIBERTY *speech* — 24
Judge Learned Hand

PRIVACY AND THE NINTH AMENDMENT *Supreme Court opinion* — 26
Justice Arthur Goldberg

EMMETT TILL *poem* — 28
James A. Emanuel

TINKER CASE GUIDES COURT AS STUDENT'S PARODY OF — 30
PRINCIPAL IS RULED PROTECTED SPEECH *news story*
and **STUDENT SPEECH CAN BE RESTRICTED** *Supreme Court opinion*
Beth Hawkins *and* Chief Justice John Roberts

REPRODUCIBLE FORMS

Shared Inquiry Discussion Guidelines   32

Building Your Answer in Shared Inquiry Discussion   34

Great Books Critical Thinking Rubric   36

About Shared Inquiry and This Guide

Welcome! This discussion guide for *Individual Rights: The Blessings of Liberty* features a selection of texts that the Great Books Foundation recommends for close reading, text-based discussion, and evidence-based writing. Great Books programs use a method of interpretive reading and discussion known as Shared Inquiry,™ which complements the critical thinking encouraged in *Individual Rights*.

Shared Inquiry is fully supportive of Common Core State Standards in both pedagogy and content. In Shared Inquiry, the leader uses open-ended questioning to help participants reach their own conclusions about challenging literature. The suggested sequence of activities—reading and asking questions, rereading and making notes, and exploring possible interpretations in discussion—mirrors the process that effective readers use with any complex text. Using Shared Inquiry, students develop the intellectual flexibility to analyze ideas and see a question from many angles. The focus on interpretation and discussion allows students at different reading levels to participate confidently and improve their critical thinking abilities.

This discussion guide includes general information about leading Shared Inquiry discussion and activities for eight selections from *Individual Rights*. For each selection, you will find a prereading question, a note prompt for the second reading, suggested discussion questions, and prompts for writing after discussion. Also included are reproducible student handout pages for use in discussion and a rubric to assess critical thinking.

Professional Learning and Online Resources

The Great Books Foundation offers a range of professional learning opportunities, including online course options and on-site consultation days tailored to individual teachers' and schools' needs. To learn more, visit < www.greatbooks.org > or call 800-222-5870.

Free resources, including downloadable materials and videos of classroom discussions are available at < www.greatbooks.org/resources >. Anyone who has taken the core Great Books professional learning courses can visit the Teacher Leaders Club at < www.greatbooks.org/tlc > for assessment tools, podcasts, videos, and special offers on classroom materials.

Scheduling Shared Inquiry Activities

In-class work on a Great Books discussion unit consists of:

- **Prereading, first reading, and sharing questions:** setting a context for reading, reading the selection aloud if possible, and identifying questions worth exploring
- **Second reading:** rereading the selection, making notes using a specific prompt, and comparing those notes with other students
- **Shared Inquiry discussion:** the central Great Books activity, in which questions about the meaning of the text are explored in depth
- **Writing after discussion:** helping students consolidate or extend their ideas about a text

The activities that lead up to Shared Inquiry discussion prepare students for the discussion by helping them develop ideas about the story and find evidence in the text to support those ideas. After the discussion, the writing activities help extend students' engagement with the text, giving them opportunities to synthesize and elaborate on their ideas.

Following are two sample weekly schedules. Longer selections may require more in-class sessions, and some activities can be assigned as homework, depending on your students' needs and the time available.

> **Great Books and Common Core**
>
> Shared Inquiry provides the essential elements that students need to meet and surpass the goals of the Common Core State Standards. Great Books activities for *Individual Rights*:
>
> - Explore complex informational texts
> - Require text-based answers
> - Focus on evidence in writing
> - Expand vocabulary
> - Build knowledge across the curriculum

Option A: Three In-Class Sessions

Session 1

- Prereading activity (optional)
- First reading
- Sharing questions

Session 2

- Second reading
- Comparing and discussing notes

Session 3

- Shared Inquiry discussion

Homework: Writing after discussion

Option B: Two In-Class Sessions

Session 1

- First reading
- Sharing questions

Homework: Second reading

Session 2

- Comparing and discussing notes
- Shared Inquiry discussion

Homework: Writing after discussion

Conducting Shared Inquiry Activities

Preparing to Conduct Shared Inquiry Activities

As a Shared Inquiry leader, you serve as the model of an involved, curious thinker. We recommend that you prepare for Shared Inquiry by doing what your students will be doing: noting your own reactions and questions on a first reading, and marking the text using a specific note prompt on a second reading. Familiarizing yourself with the interpretive issues raised by the selection in this way will enable you to help your students develop their own ideas about the text as they participate in the sequence of Great Books activities.

Prereading 10–15 minutes *(optional)*

Activity Summary: Students briefly discuss a concept relevant to the text they will be reading.

Student Learning Objective: To activate prior knowledge and provide a context for understanding a text

The activities in this guide include a topic for a brief discussion before students read the text for the first time. A prereading discussion is especially helpful if the selection is challenging or the subject matter is unfamiliar to students. Keep prereading discussions short, since the goal is to spur students' interest in the text.

First Reading *(time depends on selection length)*

Activity Summary: Students read the text or listen as it is read aloud, marking places where they have questions.

Student Learning Objective: To clarify understanding of a text by making notes and asking questions about parts of a text that prompt confusion or curiosity

We recommend reading the selection aloud, if possible. Reading aloud:

- Allows students to enjoy the selection
- Helps students take in unfamiliar vocabulary
- Gives students the model of a fluent reader using appropriate pace and expression
- Ensures that all students begin their interpretive work on an equal footing
- Leads naturally to students sharing questions about the selection

Sharing Questions 15–20 minutes

Activity Summary: Students share questions about the text.

Student Learning Objectives: To identify questions arising from a text and to begin to identify interpretive questions

After the first reading, encourage students to ask any questions they have about the selection. Try writing students' questions on the board or chart paper. Factual or vocabulary questions can be cleared up at this point, while questions reflecting students' curiosity about the meaning of the selection should be noted and saved for Shared Inquiry discussion.

Sharing questions after the first reading:

- Teaches students that their curiosity is a starting point for interpretive thinking
- Develops the habit of reflecting and questioning after reading
- Clears up initial misreadings and comprehension difficulties
- Generates questions worth exploring in discussion
- Fosters a cooperative learning atmosphere
- Helps you gauge students' understanding of the text and identify interpretive issues of interest

Second Reading *(time depends on selection length)*

Activity Summary: Students reread the selection and mark passages using a specific note prompt. Then students briefly compare and discuss their notes.

Student Learning Objectives: To reread and mark passages for deeper understanding of a text and to explore different responses to a text by explaining and comparing notes

The activities in this guide include a note prompt that highlights a key interpretive issue in the text. In reviewing students' notes with them, look for opportunities to help students become aware of and compare different reactions to the same passage.

Rereading and taking notes:

- Gives students guided practice in choosing passages for close examination
- Develops students' ability to recall and use supporting evidence for their opinions
- Enables students to draw connections as they read and recognize interpretive issues
- Helps students see that a passage can have different interpretations
- Encourages students to use notes as a way of reacting to and thinking about literature

Tips for Sharing Notes

To help your students get the most out of making and sharing notes:

- Allow time for students to discuss some of their notes, so that they see different interpretive possibilities. With a longer text, ask students to share their notes from two or three pages.
- Ask students to share not only what they marked but also why they marked it, or have them discuss their notes in pairs while you circulate, asking follow-up questions as needed.
- Ask follow-up questions such as *Why did you mark the passage that way? Did anyone else mark it that way? Did anyone mark it differently, and if so, why?* to help students understand both their thinking and that of others.

Here are examples of how two students marked a page in the "The Spirit of Liberty" by Judge Learned Hand when asked to mark with an **I** places where Hand emphasizes the importance of the **individual**, and mark with a **C** places where he emphasizes **common** purpose.

Student A

What then is the spirit of liberty? I cannot define it; I can only tell you my own faith. The spirit of liberty is the spirit which is not too sure that it is right; the spirit of liberty is <u>the spirit which seeks to understand the mind of other men and women;</u> the spirit of liberty is the spirit which weighs their interests alongside its own without bias; the spirit of liberty remembers that not even a sparrow falls to earth unheeded; the spirit of liberty is the spirit of Him who, near two thousand years ago, taught mankind that lesson it has never learned but never quite forgotten; that there may be a kingdom where the least shall be heard and considered side by side with the greatest. And now in that spirit, that spirit of an America which has never been, and which may never be; nay, <u>which never will be except as the conscience and courage of Americans create it;</u> yet in the spirit of that America which lies hidden in some form in the aspirations of us all; in <u>the spirit of that America for which our young men are at this moment fighting and dying;</u> in that spirit of liberty and of America I ask
C you to rise and with me <u>pledge our faith in the glorious destiny of our beloved country.</u>

C He sees a connection

C Everyone together creates the spirit

C Fighting for our freedom

Student B

I What then is the spirit of liberty? I cannot define it; I can only <u>tell you my own faith.</u> The spirit of liberty is the spirit which is not too sure that it is right; the spirit of liberty is the spirit which seeks to understand the mind of other men and women; the spirit of liberty is the spirit which weighs their interests alongside its own without bias; the spirit of liberty remembers that not even a sparrow falls to earth unheeded; the spirit of liberty is the spirit of Him who, near two thousand years ago, taught mankind that lesson it has never learned but never quite forgotten; that there may be <u>a kingdom where the least shall be heard and considered side by side with the greatest.</u> And now in that spirit, that spirit of an America which has never been, and which may never be; nay, <u>which never will be except as the conscience and courage of Americans create it;</u> yet in the spirit of that America which lies hidden in some form in the aspirations of us all; in the spirit of that America for which our young men are at this moment fighting and dying; in that spirit of liberty and of America I ask
C you to rise and with me <u>pledge our faith in the glorious destiny of our beloved country.</u>

I Everyone has an equal vote

I It's up to each American

Shared Inquiry Discussion 30–45 minutes

Activity Summary: Students explore the text's meaning by discussing an interpretive question.

Student Learning Objectives: To generate ideas in response to an interpretive question about a text; to support ideas and arguments with relevant evidence from the text; and to respond to the ideas, questions, and arguments of other students

In this cornerstone activity of all Great Books programs, students work together to interpret the text. Each Shared Inquiry discussion begins with independent thought: students write their own answers to an interpretive question that you pose as the focus of discussion. Then, guided by your follow-up questions, students discuss and develop their ideas, supporting their ideas with evidence from the selection.

The activities in this guide include questions for discussion. Focus questions—interpretive questions about key issues of meaning—appear in boldface type. We encourage you to use these in combination with questions generated by you or your students. Each focus question is followed by a group of related questions that can be used as follow-up questions to help students take a closer look at specific passages.

The following pages explain how to introduce students to and conduct Shared Inquiry discussion. Two handouts—Shared Inquiry Discussion Guidelines and Building Your Answer in Shared Inquiry Discussion—can be found at the back of this guide on pages 32–33 and 34–35, in reproducible format for your convenience.

Introducing Students to Shared Inquiry Discussion

To establish an atmosphere that promotes the lively exchange of ideas, arrange the room in a circle or square so that everyone can see and hear one another. If this isn't possible, encourage students to turn to look at the person talking, acknowledging one another and not just the teacher. Students should have a convenient surface for reading and writing.

To prepare students for Shared Inquiry discussion:

- Emphasize that in discussion you are not looking for a "right" answer, but are interested in exploring a question that has more than one reasonable answer based on the text. Because there is more than one reasonable answer, the objective is not to reach consensus but to help students develop their own ideas.
- Let students know that you will be asking them to explain their ideas, give evidence to support them, and respond to other students' comments.
- Encourage students to raise questions of their own and to talk to one another rather than always to you.
- Explain the discussion guidelines (pages 32–33) and the reasons for them. You may want to copy these pages for students or display the guidelines in the classroom.
- Distribute the Building Your Answer form (pages 34–35). Let students know that using the form will help them trace the progress of their ideas about a text while facilitating any writing you may assign after the discussion.

Leading Shared Inquiry Discussion

The following suggestions will help you lead the most productive Shared Inquiry discussions for your students.

Begin the discussion with a focus question and ask students to write down an answer. Review your students' questions, your notes, and the suggested questions in this guide to help you choose a focus question that has more than one reasonable answer and reflects your and your students' interests.

Giving students time before the discussion to reflect individually on the focus question lets them gather their thoughts and find evidence for their ideas. Having students write an answer on their Building Your Answer form gives them an excellent starting point for participating in the discussion and enables you to call on less vocal students knowing they have something to contribute. Students can also reflect on their answer after the discussion, considering how they have added to or changed their ideas in response to others.

Share your curiosity and enthusiasm by listening carefully and asking follow-up questions often. Your attentive listening and follow-up questioning drive and sustain effective discussion. Use follow-up questions to help students:

- **Clarify comments.** *What do you mean by that? Can you say more about that?*
- **Support ideas with evidence.** *What in the text gave you that idea? What did the author do or say that made you think so?*
- **Test and develop ideas.** *If you think that's what the author means, then why does he or she say this in the text? How does this passage in the text fit in with your idea?*
- **Respond to others.** *What do you think about what she just said? Do you agree with that idea? Does anyone have an idea we haven't heard yet?*

Return frequently to the text and the focus question. Keep the discussion grounded in the text by asking students to support their answers with evidence. Help students think about ideas in depth by asking them to explain how their comments relate to the focus question.

Encourage students to think for themselves and to speak directly to one another instead of just to you. This makes students responsible for discussion and fosters an environment of open inquiry and respect. Try to remain in the role of a neutral leader by only asking questions, and avoid answering questions or endorsing ideas with comments such as "Good idea" or "I like that."

Keep a record of the discussion. Using a seating chart to track students' participation will help you identify patterns of participation and assess students' contributions. You might make check marks next to students' names when they offer an answer and mark "NA" when a student has no answer when asked to speak.

End the discussion when your group has explored the focus question in depth. You can usually tell when your group has considered a number of answers to the focus question and most students could, if asked, provide their own "best answer" to it. You may wish to check by asking, *Are there any different ideas we haven't heard yet? Is there any other part of the text we should look at before wrapping up?* Remind students that they do not need to reach a consensus, because the text supports multiple interpretations.

Writing After Discussion

Activity Summary: Students write in response to a question or prompt about the text.

Student Learning Objectives: To develop a thesis in response to a text and support that thesis with appropriate evidence from the text and other sources; to extend students' thinking about the ideas raised in the selection

The activities in this guide include prompts for writing and reflection after discussion. After participating in Shared Inquiry discussion, students are well prepared to consolidate or extend their responses to a text in writing. In addition to writing on one of the topics in this guide, students can consult their completed Building Your Answer form and use their answer to the focus question as the thesis of an essay.

Writing after discussion:

- Gives students practice in systematically articulating, supporting, and developing their ideas
- Stimulates original thought and encourages students to connect what they read to their own experiences and opinions
- Helps students build a commitment to reading and critical thinking by continuing their thoughtful engagement with a selection's ideas

Assessment and Reflection

Assessment

If you assign a participation grade, keeping a seating chart will help you record students' oral work for later marking. Comparing your notes from week to week will help you give students feedback on their progress, individually or as a group.

The writing prompts lend themselves to extended written responses, which can be graded like other essays. You can also evaluate the written work students do in preparation for discussion, including their questions and notes, and their Building Your Answer in Shared Inquiry Discussion forms. You may wish to ask students to submit a portfolio of their written work on a selection of their choice or from selections covered over the course of the semester.

The Great Books Critical Thinking Rubric on pages 36–37 is a detailed outline of the critical thinking skills developed in Great Books programs. Applying the rubric to students' responses in discussion as well as to their written work will give you more complete and dependable information. To use the rubric to assess critical thinking, follow these steps:

- Prior to Shared Inquiry discussion, choose one to three students to assess. As your comfort level in leading discussions grows, you may wish to increase the number of students you assess.
- After the discussion, record notes about the thinking skills of those students you are assessing. Use the notes on your seating chart to recall discussion responses. (You may also wish to record the discussions for assessment purposes.)

- Flesh out your notes about each student by reviewing their written work, including the Building Your Answer form.
- Assign separate grades for idea, evidence, and response, or grade for just one objective. Due to the collaborative nature of Shared Inquiry, a student's contributions may pertain to only one area.
- Give students feedback by sharing the rubric with them and offering suggestions for improvement.

Reflection

To help students reflect on their own learning, after every two or three discussions ask them to share their thoughts on how the discussions are going and how they might be improved. Help the class set specific goals for improvement in areas such as supporting their opinions with evidence from the text, staying focused on the meaning of the text under discussion, and speaking directly to other students rather than just to the teacher.

Online Resources
- www.greatbooks.org/assessmenttools/ for grade-specific assessment tools
- www.greatbooks.org/links-for-teachers/ for teacher resources
- www.greatbooks.org/commoncore/ for more on how Great Books programs and the Shared Inquiry method meet Common Core State Standards
- www.greatbooks.org for additional assessment and reflection resources

George Washington and the Touro Synagogue

Moses Seixas and George Washington

and

Jefferson and the "Wall of Separation"

Thomas Jefferson

Prereading

Why do you think the First Amendment contains both an establishment clause ("Congress shall make no law respecting an establishment of religion") and a free exercise clause ("or prohibiting the free exercise thereof") pertaining to religion?

Second Reading

Mark with a **C** places where Washington and Jefferson make statements based on laws and the **Constitution**; mark with an **N** places where Washington and Jefferson make statements based on a **natural order**.

Interpretive Questions for Discussion

Why do both Washington and Jefferson refer to a higher authority in their letters?

1. Why does Washington qualify his statement that "we cannot fail . . . to become a great and happy people" by writing, "If we have wisdom to make the best use of the advantages with which we are now favored"?

2. When Washington refers to a "just administration of a good Government," is he talking about something he thinks already exists, or something he hopes for?

3. When Washington states that "the father of all mercies" will make us "everlastingly happy," why does he add "in his own due time and way"?
4. Why is it important to Washington that in America rights are not granted by the indulgence of one class of people to another?
5. Why does Jefferson make a point of saying that the praise he received from the Connecticut Baptists in their letter to him gave him "the highest satisfaction"? Why does he tell the Baptists that he reciprocates their kind prayers?
6. What does it mean to build a "wall of separation between church and State"?
7. Why is Jefferson convinced that a citizen "has no natural right in opposition to his social duties?"
8. Does Jefferson's assertion that the law reaches "actions only, and not opinions" derive from his belief in the Constitution or a person's natural rights?

Writing After Discussion

Have students write an essay, using evidence from the text, to support their answer to the focus question in discussion, or use one of the following:

1. What is the "enlarged and liberal policy" that Washington says is worthy of imitation?
2. Compare Washington's letter to the Touro Synagogue with Jefferson's letter to the Connecticut Baptists. Which letter gives greater assurance of religious freedom?
3. Research and read the complete texts of both Seixas's welcome greeting and Washington's letter in response. To what extent does Washington address Seixas's concerns?

Thoughts That We Hate

Anthony Lewis

Prereading

What restrictions, if any, should be placed on freedom of speech?

Second Reading

Mark with an **R** laws or court cases that seem to **restrict** freedom of speech; mark with a **P** laws or court cases that seem to **protect** freedom of speech.

Interpretive Questions for Discussion

How does Lewis's statement that speech should be punishable if it "urges terrorist violence to an audience some of whose members are ready to act on the urging" differ from the restrictions already placed on speech by constitutional law?

1. Why does Lewis distinguish speech that inspires "acts of mass murder or terrorism" from other types of violence?

2. What does Lewis mean when he says, "The generalized smear of hate speech . . . does not lend itself to the factual analysis contemplated by these later [court] decisions"?

3. Does Lewis base his argument that we should be able to restrict speech that advocates terrorist violence to people "who are ready to act on the urging" more on legal and constitutional grounds or moral and ethical grounds?

4. How does Lewis's point that we live in an age "when words have inspired acts of mass murder and terrorism" support his argument? Is Lewis saying this is a new development in history?

5. Why does Lewis review court cases that bear on hate speech to make his point? Does his review of freedom of speech laws in other countries help make his case?

Writing After Discussion

Have students write an essay, using evidence from the text, to support their answer to the focus question in discussion, or use one of the following:

1. Do you agree with Justice Brandeis in his opinion in *Whitney v. California* when he writes, "Discussion affords ordinarily adequate protection against the dissemination of noxious doctrine"?

2. Do you agree that freedom of speech laws in America are based on "an inveterate social and historical optimism"? Is the optimism warranted?

3. Should the ability to reach vast audiences through social media today make us more inclined to restrict hate speech or to protect it?

The Spirit of Liberty
Judge Learned Hand

Prereading

Why do hundreds of thousands of immigrants seek to become United States citizens each year?

Second Reading

Mark with an **I** places where Hand emphasizes the importance of the **individual**; mark with a **C** places where he emphasizes **common** purpose.

Interpretive Questions for Discussion

Why does Hand say that he cannot define the spirit of liberty, but can only talk about his "own faith"?

1. Does Hand think that the spirit of liberty in America is founded on individual legal rights or "faith in a common purpose"? What is the "common purpose" that Hand says the new American citizens are there to affirm?

2. Why does Hand, a federal judge, say that hopes of securing liberty through constitutions, laws, and courts are "false hopes"?

3. Why is the freedom to do as one likes a denial of liberty?

4. Why does Hand say that the spirit of liberty "is not too sure that it is right"?

5. According to Hand, how is the spirit of liberty the same as that which "seeks to understand the mind of other men and women"?

6. What does Hand mean when he says that the spirit of America "has never been, and . . . never will be except as the conscience and courage of Americans create it"?

7. What are "the aspirations of us all" in which the spirit of America lies hidden? Does Hand suggest that the spirit of liberty is something Americans possess, or something they strive for?

Writing After Discussion

Have students write an essay, using evidence from the text, to support their answer to the focus question in discussion, or use one of the following:

1. What does the spirit of America mean to you?
2. To what extent does living in America afford you with freedom from oppression, freedom from want, and the freedom to be yourself?
3. Research the requirements for becoming a naturalized citizen of the United States. Should people who are citizens by birth be required to know as much about the American form of government as naturalized citizens?

Privacy and the Ninth Amendment

Justice Arthur Goldberg

Prereading

What makes a right "fundamental"?

Second Reading

Mark with an **F** words or phrases that help you understand what the justices mean when they say a right is **fundamental**.

Interpretive Questions for Discussion

Why do the justices conclude that the right of privacy in marital relations is a "fundamental and basic" right of American citizens?

1. If we were to allow infringement of the right of marital privacy because that right is not explicit in the Constitution, why would we then be ignoring the Ninth Amendment?
2. To what are the justices referring when they look to the "traditions and [collective] conscience of our people" to determine whether a right is fundamental? What does it mean that a principle is "rooted" in the nation's collective conscience?
3. How does the right of privacy emanate "from the totality of the constitutional scheme under which we live"?
4. Why does Justice Brandeis write that the right to be left alone is "the most comprehensive of rights and the right most valued by civilized men"?
5. What does it mean to say that "the home derives its preeminence as the seat of family life"? Why is this important to the argument about privacy in marital relations?

Writing After Discussion

Have students write an essay, using evidence from the text, to support their answer to the focus question in discussion, or use one of the following:

1. Do you agree with Justice Brandeis that the right to be let alone is the "most valued" individual right? What are your most valued individual rights?

2. In addition to a right to privacy in a marriage, in what other areas should Americans have a right to privacy? What makes some rights more fundamental than others?

3. Read "Putting the Second Amendment Second" by Akhil Reed Amar and compare Justice Goldberg's use of the Ninth Amendment to support the right to privacy with Amar's use of it to support a right to bear arms. Which argument is stronger? Would Justice Goldberg agree with Amar's claim that the right to bear arms is a "fundamental right" protected by the Ninth Amendment?

Emmett Till

James A. Emanuel

Prereading

Should race ever be a consideration in selecting a jury in a criminal case?

Second Reading

Underline words or phrases where Emanuel uses figurative language to create a vivid picture.

Interpretive Questions for Discussion

According to the poet, why won't Emmett be still?

1. Why does Emmett float "Round the darkness, / Edging through / The silent chill"?
2. Who is the speaker of the poem? To whom is the request "Tell me, please" spoken?
3. Why is the story of the River Boy called a "bedtime story"?
4. What are the treasures in which the River Boy is eternally swimming?
5. Why does the poem end with the River Boy being "Necklaced in / A coral toy"?

Writing After Discussion

Have students write an essay, using evidence from the text, to support their answer to the focus question in discussion, or use one of the following:

1. Should the formal apology offered by Tallahatchie County in the Emmett Till case provide solace to Emmett's family, or is it too little too late?

2. In cases where a clear injustice has occurred, do you think it is possible to adequately correct the injustice for those involved? Who bears ultimate responsibility for pursuing justice in such cases?

3. Research the law regarding jury selection in a criminal jury trial. Should attorneys be allowed to exclude prospective jurors from a jury because their race is the same as or different from the defendant's?

4. Why might a writer choose to express his or her thoughts in a poem like this instead of an essay?

Tinker Case Guides Court as Student's Parody of Principal Is Ruled Protected Speech
Beth Hawkins

and

Student Speech Can Be Restricted
Chief Justice John Roberts

Prereading

What restrictions, if any, should be placed on a student's constitutional right to free speech at school?

Second Reading

Mark with an **S** places where the author indicates that students enjoy the **same** First Amendment rights as adults; mark with an **R** places where the author indicates that students' First Amendment rights are more **restricted**.

Interpretive Questions for Discussion

Considering the rulings in *Tinker v. Des Moines Independent Community School District*, *Layshock v. Hermitage School District*, and *Morse v. Frederick*, how do the three cases illustrate the evolving nature of constitutional law?

1. What do the courts mean by "disrupting the education process"?

2. What does Hawkins think is the nature of "Layshock's misbehavior"?
3. Why does Hawkins think that Layshock should not suffer legal consequences but still deserves to be punished?
4. According to Chief Justice Roberts, what are the "special characteristics of the school environment" that are relevant in determining students' First Amendment rights?
5. What is "political speech"? Why is the armband worn by Mary Beth Tinker protected political speech while "BONG HiTS 4 JESUS" is not?

Writing After Discussion

Have students write an essay, using evidence from the text, to support their answer to the focus question in discussion, or use one of the following:

1. Given Chief Justice Roberts's opinion in *Morse v. Frederick*, how would you advise a court to decide a similar case in which the student's banner advocated decriminalizing marijuana?
2. You are a high school principal dealing with a situation in which a student running for student counsel registers a complaint because an opponent's stump speech, delivered at a school-sponsored event, contained several exaggerations and misleading statements about the speaker's accomplishments. Describe any issues relating to students' First Amendment rights and explain how you would handle the problem.
3. Write a set of guidelines for unacceptable content for your school newspaper, consistent with the First Amendment rights of students in a school setting.

Shared Inquiry Discussion Guidelines

Come to the discussion with your book, a pen or pencil, a notebook, and an open mind. In Shared Inquiry discussion, everyone, including the leader, considers a question with more than one reasonable answer and weighs the evidence for different answers. The goal of the discussion is for each of you to develop an answer that satisfies you personally.

Following these guidelines will make for a better discussion:

★ **Read the text twice before participating in the discussion.** This ensures that everyone is prepared to talk about the ideas in the selection.

★ **Discuss only the text that everyone has read.** This keeps the discussion focused on understanding the selection.

★ **Support your ideas with evidence from the text.** This enables everyone to weigh textual support for different ideas and to choose intelligently among them.

★ **Listen to other participants, respond to them directly, and ask them questions.** Shared Inquiry is about the give-and-take of ideas, and speaking directly to other group members, not always to the leader, makes the discussion livelier and more authentic.

★ **Expect the leader to only ask questions, rather than offer opinions or answers.** The leader's role is to listen and ask questions in order to help participants develop their own ideas, with everyone, including the leader, gaining a new understanding in the process.

Copyright © 2012 by The Great Books Foundation

Building Your Answer
in Shared Inquiry Discussion

Name: _____

Selection: _____

Focus question: _____
_____
_____
_____

Your answer before discussion (include something from the text that supports your answer): _____
_____
_____
_____

How did the discussion affect your answer? Did it change your mind or provide additional support for your answer? Did it make you aware of other issues? _____

_____
_____
_____

Your answer after discussion: _____

_____
_____
_____

What in the selection helped you decide on this answer? _____

_____
_____

Great Books
Critical Thinking Rubric

Performance Level		Idea: Generating an Interpretation
7	Extends Interpretation	Extends ideas to interpret text as a whole • Identifies themes, author's perspective • Goes beyond the question, widens the issues under discussion
6	Builds Interpretation	Elaborates on own idea • Defines terms, explores implications • Resolves inconsistencies
5	Explains Answer	Explains how an idea answers the question • Relates actions, characters, statements to each other • To clarify, spells out assumptions, relates them to the question
4	Understands Issues	Fully understands the interpretive issue • Infers motives and causes, addresses the question directly • To clarify, tells more about the answer
3	Recognizes Alternatives	Asserts a considered answer, aware of alternative ideas • May hesitate between answers • To clarify, paraphrases answer
2	Offers Simple, Quick Answers	Gives a quick, simple answer to the question • All-or-nothing, snap judgment • To clarify, repeats answer
1	Begins to Answer	Talks about the text without addressing the question

Copyright © 2012 by The Great Books Foundation

Evidence: Using Support from the Text	Response: Listening and Responding to Others
Brings together evidence from whole text • Uses both major incidents and subtle details • Compares and weighs evidence	Seeks out other students' ideas • Asks questions to clarify other students' ideas and suggests possibilities • Suggests support for others' ideas
Builds case from several different passages • Retraces process of thinking • Continues to add evidence during discussion	Incorporates other students' ideas and evidence • Agrees or disagrees with specific parts • Follows whole discussion
Explains how a passage supports an idea • Explores meanings, connotations for relevant words, phrases • Sees when evidence works against own idea	Explains and gives reasons for agreement and disagreement • Critiques or supports other students' ideas • Asks other students simple questions
Understands the need for evidence • Spontaneously looks back into the text • Focuses on relevant sentences	Understands and roughly summarizes other students' ideas • May be convinced by others • Follows other students' counterarguments
Supports an answer against an alternative answer • Locates relevant major passages • Reads or recounts whole passages	Recognizes alternative answers and agrees or disagrees simply
Tends not to volunteer support; offers support only when asked • Recalls major text facts • Considers answer self-evident	Reacts briefly or quickly to other students' answers without talking about them
May retell the story or give an opinion about something mentioned in the text	Allows others to speak without interrupting

Copyright © 2012 by The Great Books Foundation

Notes

Notes

Notes